Giova Press, PO Box 7775 #20915, San Francisco, CA 94120
www.giovapress.com

Publisher's Cataloging-in-Publication data

Kriss, Jane.
Next Stop Sausalito / Jane Kriss
Description: Sausalito, CA : Giova Press, 2016.
p. cm.
ISBN 978-1-68418-526-9 (hardcover)

Subjects: LCSH: Sausalito (Calif.)--Description and travel. | San Francisco Bay Area (Calif.)--
Description and travel. | California, Northern--Description and travel. | Gift books. | Illustrated
books. | BISAC: HISTORY / United States / State & Local / West (AK, CA, CO, HI, ID, MT, NV,
UT, WY). | TRAVEL / United States / West / Pacific (AK, CA, HI, OR, WA).
Classification: LCC F869.S59 K75 2016 (print) | LCC F869.S59 (ebook) | DDC 979.4/62--dc23.

Library of Congress Control Number: 2016918242
First Edition

For Tycho and Vera Jane

Next Stop
SAUSALITO

WRITTEN AND ILLUSTRATED

BY JANE KRISS

Sausalito is where the Golden Gate Bridge lands after taking off from the city of San Francisco.

Of course the Golden Gate Bridge was not always there. It wasn't built until 1937, about 3000 years after the Coastal Miwok first came, naming their village Liwanclowa.

Sausalito is often said to be the closest thing the
United States has to an Italian hill town.

Two million visitors arrive here from all around the world every year.

Half of them are migratory birds.

The migratory birds and year-'round birds play well together...

...and so do the toursts and the local residents.

If someone is walking a dog, they probably live here.
If they look sleepy it might be because the fog horns on
the Golden Gate Bridge kept them up last night.

If someone is looking at a map or taking a selfie they are probably a tourist.

Don't ask them for directions.

But you might have a chance to practice your Italian, Swahili, or Russian.

Some visitors come by bus,
some by bicycle, some by car, and some fly.

But the best way to get to Sausalito from San Francisco is to hop on the ferry.

You can also take it back, unless you would rather walk or taxi across the Golden Gate Bridge.

The first ferryboat in Sausalito, about 150 years ago, was named the Princess. And that's how Princess Street, one of the town's first two streets, got its name.

When the railroads were built and people and lumber began riding trains down from the north, the Sausalito ferries became very important. Since the Golden Gate Bridge wasn't yet built, they were the only way to get to San Francisco, which was already a big, fast-growing city.

If you miss the ferry and come by car, you can park in a parking lot and use a solar-powered payment machine.

I ♥ 94965

The parking control officers in Sausalito are very friendly, and they are good at their jobs. Even residents are not allowed to park their cars on the street for more than 72 hours.

Guess how long you can park your boat in the Bay without a special permit? Yup, 72 hours.

The first thing you will probably see in Sausalito is Viña del Mar Park.

The park is named after Sausalito's Sister City in Chile.
And if you visit Viña del Mar in Chile, you will notice that there is a lagoon there named Sausalito. Sausalito has two more sister cities — one in Japan and one in Portugal.

The elephant statues and the fountain in Viña del Mar Park arrived by ferry from San Francisco, just as you may have, but they came more than 100 years ago. They had been made for the 1915 Panama Pacific Fair and Exposition but needed a permanent home.

They weren't built to last, though, and when Jumbo crumbled 20 years later, both he and Pee Wee were re-cast out of concrete.

December seems to be the only month they dress up.

There may be even more boats in Sausalito than tourists and birds.
Boats and floating homes fill nine harbors and marinas.

Galilee Harbor even has its own greenhouses.

There are working boats...

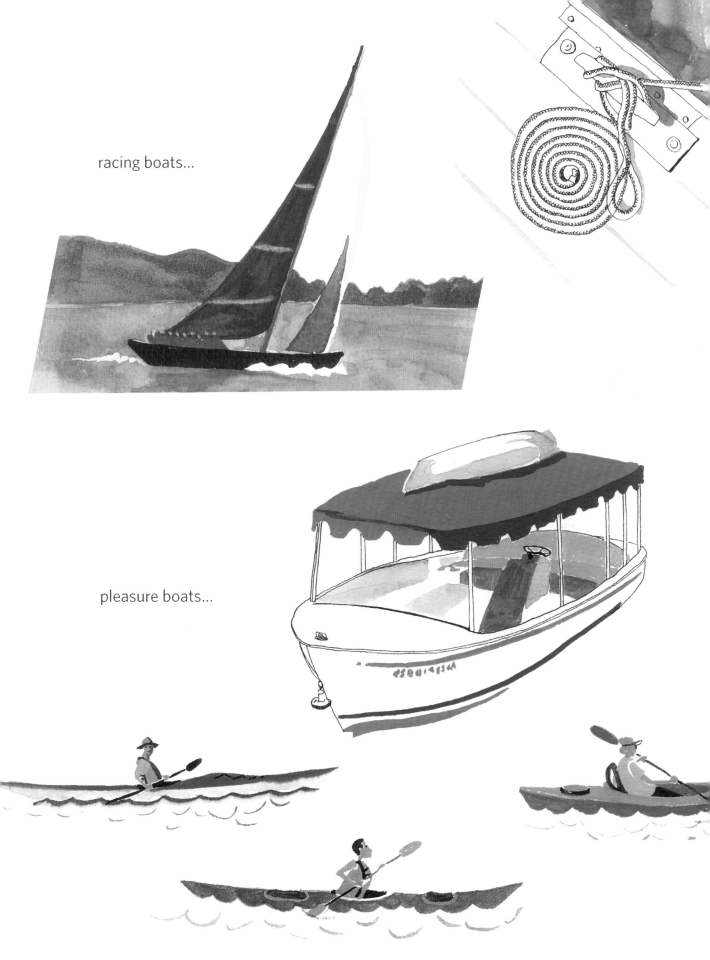

racing boats...

pleasure boats...

These lockers are used by boat owners for storing paint and maintenance supplies. Oh, also party drinks.

teaching boats...

historic teaching boats...

An updated copy of The Galilee, an
1891 brigantine ship, is being built in
Sausalito right now. It will be 132 feet
long, with a 100 foot tall mast.
Kids will be able to learn all about our
oceans and navigation while on board.

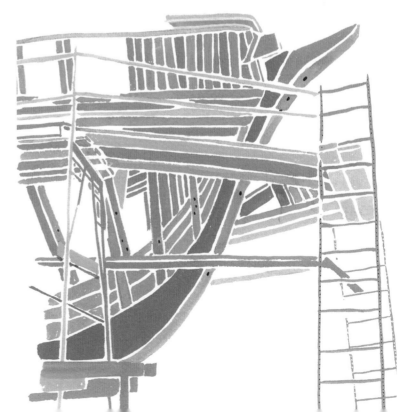

One of the oldest floating homes, The Vallejo, is a converted ferry boat.
It's where the sidewalk ends — in fact, author Shel Silverstein once lived there.

...and sunken boats.

The two ends of The Galilee are on display in San Francisco, but its middle is still at the bottom of the Bay next to Galilee Harbor in Sausalito.

Boats that are anchored away from the docks are called anchor-outs.

People who live on anchor-outs get to shore in rowboats. They often keep a bike at the nearest dock for getting around town, since rowboats don't do well on city streets...

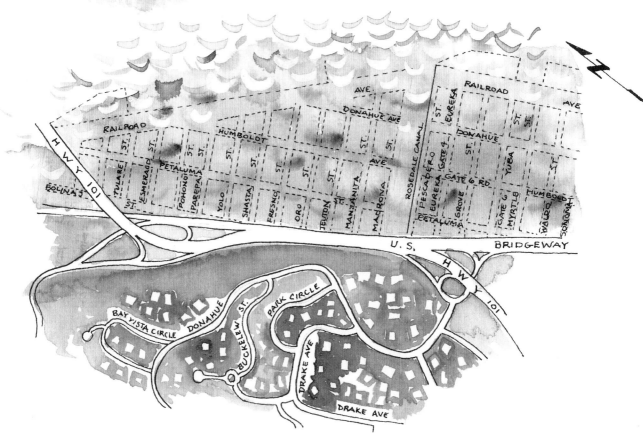

...unless they are the Sausalito streets that are underwater, like Myrtle Street or Donahue.

The underwater streets aren't actually there. They only exist on the government maps but are important for agreeing where the floating homes can dock. As the water level of the Bay rises along with our oceans, there may be even more streets under water. This already happens during the super-high King Tides.

With so much water activity, the Sausalito Emergency Teams need to be prepared to get wet. You may never have seen a fire department truck with a surfboard on top!

The Search and Rescue Team members are trained to help people and animals in water-related emergencies — in the bay, the ocean, rivers and floods.

And they have a very fancy mailbox.

In Sausalito not all the boats
are in the water...

and not all the houses are on land.

These are technically called floating homes, since they don't have sails or motors. If they need to be moved, a boat will tow them.

One of the floating homes, not far from the ferry landing, is called The Taj. Of course it is not quite as large as the real Taj Mahal. You will have to visit India to see that one.

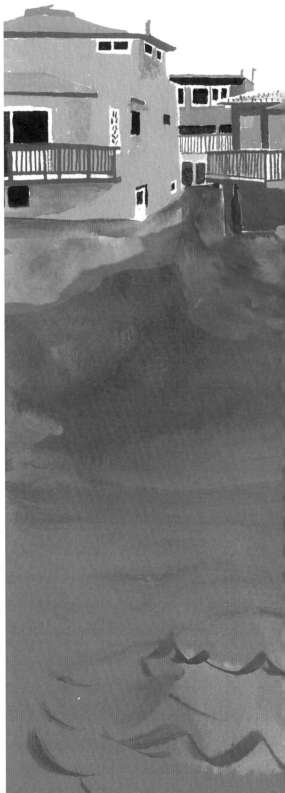

Farther up the bay you will find over 400 more houseboats.

Sausalito is not only a good place to sail boats —
it's always been a great place to build and repair them.

This is a San Francisco Fire Department boat on shore,
getting fixed up in one of Sausalito's shipyards.

During World War II ninety-three ships were built here in only three and a half years. 15 Liberty ships (cargo ships), 16 fleet oilers (for fuel and supplies transport), and 62 tankers (also for fuel). The tankers were over 500 feet long.

One of the office buildings for the war-time shipyard now houses 230 artist studios. Several weekends a year you can visit and see what they are making.

Not far from the artists' building you will find the Bay Model.
It's a huge model of the Bay Area waterways — all the deltas, estuaries, rivers, lagoons, tributaries, bays, canals, channels, coves and straits. The Bay Model was created in 1957 to test the wisdom of building a giant dam in the bay.
Happily, it did not pass the wisdom test!

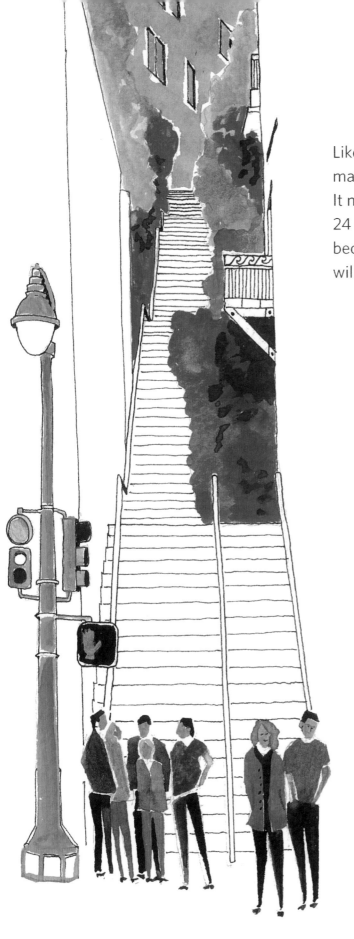

Like most hill towns, Sausalito has many staircases, both inside and out. It might take you all day to find all 24 of the shortcuts between blocks, because some are well hidden, but you will see a few right away.

If you make it to the top you will leave the tourists behind and see where the locals are perched. There are also some architectural treasures you might stumble upon.

The Sausalito Woman's Club building was designed in 1918 by Julia Morgan, California's first licensed female architect. She designed about 800 buildings, but only three in Sausalito.

For a while it looked as if one of her projects, Hearst Castle,
would be built here, but not everyone was excited about that
idea, and it was built farther down the coast,
in San Simeon, California.

The Sausalito Presbyterian Church
is believed to have been designed by Julia
Morgan's mentor, the architect Bernard
Maybeck, early in his career,
before he had his own firm.

You may even run across a local restaurant's vegetable garden.

Or the bench dedicated to the poet Daniel O'Connell.

Whether you are on the water
or on the hill, there are beautiful
views in all directions.

Sometimes the view of San Francisco looks like this...

...and sometimes it looks like this...

...and sometimes like this.

The fog bank that comes through the Golden Gate and heads straight across the Bay to Berkeley is called the Berkeley Tongue.

On a clear night it looks like this.

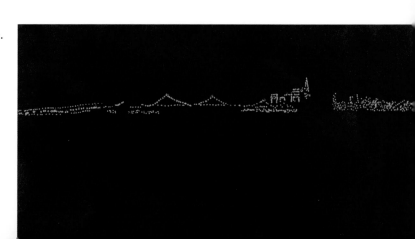

Pelicans seem to agree with people on where best to enjoy the views.

You will find someone else enjoying the view if you walk along the sidewalk toward San Francisco — a sea lion made by the artist Al Sybrian.

Sometimes swimming and sometimes sitting on the rocks, depending on how high the tide is, the Sea Lion is a reminder that there are thousands of sea lions and seals in the bay, even if they don't always pop their heads above water while we're watching.

The Marine Mammal Center, over the hill on the ocean side of Sausalito, rescues and cures injured ones. California sea lions are considered the smartest variety of seals.

Also facing the view, on the other side of the street, stand two of what used to be called the Three Sisters. They are named Lolita and Lucretia. The third sister, Lurline, was torn down in 1914 to make way for a new telephone exchange building.

If Lolita and Lucretia look like they're dressed up with nowhere to go, it's because the parties come to them. Sausalito has always been a great place for festivals and celebrations.

There's the Sausalito Art Festival,

The Classic Car Show,

Jazz and Blues by the Bay,
Sausalito Floating Homes Tour,
Herring Festival,
Galilee Harbor Maritime Day,
Sausalito Film Festival,
Sausalito Chili Cook-off,
and Gingerbread House Competition.

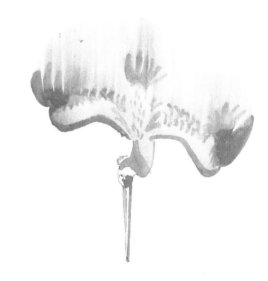

At the Herring Festival people grill their herring, but the
Brown Pelicans eat them raw after a dramatic nose dive
into the water. The deeper the fish, the higher the dive.

Sausalitans also love a parade!

The July 4th Parade, Picnic and Fireworks,
Easter Parade and Egg Hunt,
Halloween Parade,
Festa do Espirito Santo, and the
Winterfest and Lighted Boat Parade.

All the parades go down Caledonia Street, past City Hall.

This is the heart of the "real" Sausalito. The building was a school before it became the City Hall and the Sausalito Branch of the Marin County Library. It's a good place to get a building permit. And — especially if you live on a boat — a good place to stay warm with a good book on a stormy day.

Where there are parades there is music!

Sausalito may seem like a peaceful place,
but almost every night there is music somewhere in town.
Mostly jazz and rock, although sometimes there is
afternoon opera singing in the park.

During the concert you might take
a break to hunt for crabs or play a
game of Checkers.

Dozens of bands have recorded their music in Sausalito, mostly at a studio called The Record Plant. It was in operation for almost four decades. The playful front doors were carved by the local sculptor and carpenter, Dave Richards.

There are many good stories about The Record Plant,

but possibly the best one is that John Lennon and Yoko Ono came to the opening costume party dressed as trees.

Sausalito is very lucky to still have lots of real trees.

At Fort Baker they make sure to only grow plants from the seeds of the plants that are already there. That way the ecosystem won't be upset by any new-comers.

It looks almost the same now as it did 100 years ago when the Fort was built,

only now it's a hotel...
and there is a Children's Discovery Museum next door.

So now I'm wondering —
what will YOU discover in Sausalito?

PUBLIC SHORE

CAT CROSSING

BIKES

FERRY PASSENGERS ONLY

BIKES OTHER SIDE

TSUNAMI HAZARD ZONE

IN CASE OF EARTHQUAKE GO
TO HIGH GROUND OR INLAND

PARKING AHEAD

NO DUMPING
DRAINS TO BAY

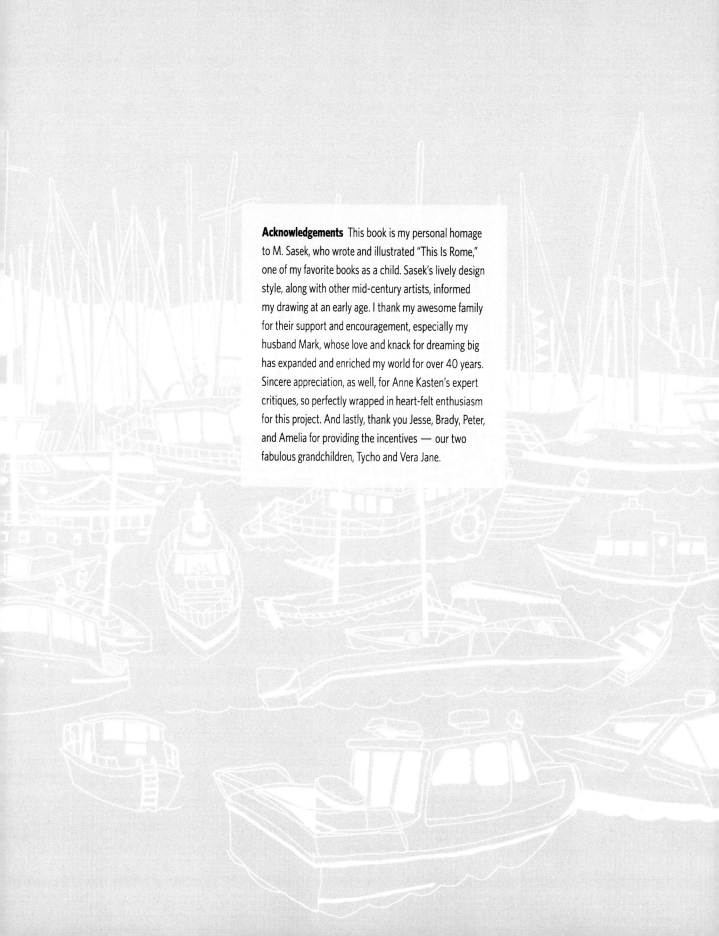

Acknowledgements This book is my personal homage to M. Sasek, who wrote and illustrated "This Is Rome," one of my favorite books as a child. Sasek's lively design style, along with other mid-century artists, informed my drawing at an early age. I thank my awesome family for their support and encouragement, especially my husband Mark, whose love and knack for dreaming big has expanded and enriched my world for over 40 years. Sincere appreciation, as well, for Anne Kasten's expert critiques, so perfectly wrapped in heart-felt enthusiasm for this project. And lastly, thank you Jesse, Brady, Peter, and Amelia for providing the incentives — our two fabulous grandchildren, Tycho and Vera Jane.

CPSIA information can be obtained
at www.ICGtesting.com
Printed in the USA
BVXC01n0300231216
471669BV00002B/2